Jesus Is My Superhero: I Want To Be Like Him

Dr. Celeste Blow

Written Words Publishing LLC
14189 E Dickinson Drive, Unit F
Aurora, CO 80014
www.writtenwordspublishing.com

Published by Written Words Publishing LLC July 1, 2023

ISBN: 978-1-961610-02-6 (hardcover)
ISBN: 978-1-961610-04-0 (softcover)
ISBN: 978-1-961610-03-3 (eBook)

Library of Congress Control Number: 2023911758

Cover Design by Dr. Celeste Blow

Illustrations created and/or arranged by Dr. Celeste Blow and Denise Blow-King using Videoleap by Lightricks Ltd. All images are used under license and permission from Videoleap by Lightricks Ltd.

Manufactured and printed in the United States of America

Dedication

This book is dedicated to God, Our Heavenly Father, Adonai, for creating us, loving us and for sending Jesus (Yeshua) in a human body like ours to redeem us. This book is also dedicated to Jesus. We love You, Jesus. Thank You for coming to Earth to talk to mankind about God's plan of salvation through You. Thank You, Jesus, for loving us, dying for us, sending the Holy Spirit to help us, and preparing a place for us. You are indeed the superhero of this family.

Dr. Celeste Blow's Family
Lower left to right: August, Winter and Michael
Upper left to right: Michelle, Judah, Malcolm, and Harmonii

Hello, my name is Judah. With the help of some friends, I will tell you about my superhero. His name is Jesus. Some people call Him Yeshua because that is His Hebrew name. He came to Earth from Heaven. He was born from Virgin Mary. He died on the cross, and three days later, he rose from the grave, ascended to Heaven, and will come back to Earth to rescue true believers.

1

In the beginning of the Bible, God made Adam from the dust of the Earth. He is a man. He is a male like me.

God made Eve. She is a woman. She is a female like my sister, Harmonii.

2

Adam and Eve lived in paradise. God told them not to touch or eat the fruit from the tree which gives the knowledge of good and evil. One day, the devil appeared as a snake and wanted to get Eve in trouble. He told her to eat fruit from the tree and she did. Then she gave the fruit to Adam. They disobeyed God and God sent them out of paradise.

Sin entered the Earth through Adam. God has an order. Adam's sin activated the order of God that states sins must be punished.

The Bible says in Romans 5:19, "One man disobeyed God, and many became sinners. But in the same way, one man obeyed God, and many will be made right." Through Adam, sin entered the world. Jesus took away the sin of the world! That is why we need Jesus. He came in God's order to make right what Adam did wrong.

In John 3:16, Jesus said, "For God loved the world so much that he gave his only Son. God gave his Son so that whoever believes in him may not be lost, but have eternal life." Salvation is a free gift from God! Do you want that free gift from God?

Jesus is my superhero. I want to be like Him. He has the whole world in His hands, and He loves the world and everyone in it. I want to love everyone too. Jesus sees everything we say and do. So, say kind words and be good.

Jesus loves all children of the world. We should love God with all our heart, mind, and soul, and our neighbors as ourselves. Jesus said we should love and forgive each other. We should play nice and be kind to other children.

Jesus is real! In the Bible, Psalm 91:11 states, "He has put his angels in charge of you. They will watch over you wherever you go." His presence is in and with us. We should pray this for everyone we know.

Do you know how to pray? Just close your eyes, look towards Heaven and say, "Lord, I pray Psalm 91 for angelic assistance and protection for mommy, daddy, my grandparents, my brother and sister, my entire family, neighbors, friends, and even my enemies. In Jesus' Name. Amen."

Batman is not real. Jesus is real and He is my superhero. He does miracles like waking us up to see another day and He rose from the dead. He also made other people rise from their graves with His superpower.

Superman is not real. Jesus is real and He is my superhero. He is God's son who died and rose three days later so we can be forgiven of our sins. All we have to do is pray and confess, "Jesus is Lord," and ask in His name.

Spiderman is not real. Jesus is real and He is my superhero. He has the power to walk on water. When He commands the oceans, wind and storms to be peaceful, they obey. Read Mark 4:35-41. All we have to do is have faith. Jesus will give the angels a command to pick up all worthy Christians and meet Him in the air. Then we will all go to Heaven and see the place Jesus prepared for us.

I could be the king of Africa. More than anything, I want to be like Jesus. He is the King of Kings and Lord of Lords.

I could grow up and be an astronaut. More than anything, I want to be like my superhero, Jesus. He made Heaven, angels, Earth, and all the planets and everything in them. He is ruler of the universe.

I could grow up and be a billionaire. More than anything, I want to tell people about my superhero, Jesus. Heaven is His home and Earth is His footstool. I will let my friends tell you how to make Jesus your superhero too!

Harmonii tells August, "Jesus is my superhero and He can be your superhero too. When you ask Him to have mercy and forgive you of your sins, His power will help you and live in you. The Bible states in Romans 10:9-10 we must:

1. Confess we have done bad things and ask our heavenly Father to forgive us in Jesus' (Yeshua's) name.

2. Believe in our hearts that Jesus rose from the grave. We must confess, 'Jesus is Lord and my redeeming Savior.'

3. Live right and not do bad things.

The good news is angels will rejoice and will write your name in a special book in Heaven."

August asked, "Will my name be written in a book in Heaven?"

Harmonii said, "Yes, it is called the Lamb's Book of Life. It means you are a citizen of Heaven. Things on Earth are going to get worse, and Jesus will come to rescue everyone who is worthy and whose names are in Heaven."

"Wow," said August, "Can I pray to receive Jesus now? I want Him to be my superhero and rescue me too."

"Yes," said Harmonii, "Let's pray."

Harmonii said, "August, just repeat these words after me."

"Ok," said August.

"Dear Lord of Lords and King of Kings, Jesus (Yeshua), I ask You to have mercy and forgive me for the bad things I have said, done, or thought about. Help me to be good and be obedient to my parents. I believe Jesus rose from the dead and I believe in my heart that Jesus is Lord. I receive the Holy Spirit now to be within me and with me. Thank You for Your angels who protect me and write my name in Your special book in Heaven. I will read and live according to the Bible. In Jesus' (Yeshua's) name. Amen."

"Yeah," said August, "I am a citizen of Heaven and my name is in God's special book! Jesus is my superhero and He lives in me. I am now worthy to go with Jesus when He returns to Earth. The angels will know because my name is written down in Heaven. Thanks for telling me about Jesus!"

Harmonii said, "You are welcome. Now, you have to tell everyone you know."

I am just a boy who wants to be like Jesus. That is why I asked Him into my heart and asked Him to be with me at all times. Tell someone today about Jesus and how He can be their superhero too.

Jesus is my superhero. I asked Him to come to live inside of me.
He has all power in His hands. He created the planets, people,
plants, and animals. He walked on water, raised the dead, and
performed many other miracles. I thank Jesus for holding the
entire creation of the universe together.

When He returns to Earth, many people will be taken to Heaven and many will be left behind. Live for Jesus while you can. Nothing is more important than where you will spend eternity. When a person's heartbeat stops forever starts, and there are two options of where they will spend eternity. There is a place better than Earth. It is called Heaven. There is also a place where bad people go. It is worse than Earth. It is called hell. Jesus is the only way to keep people from going to that terrible place. Live for Jesus and tell others about Him and you will be rewarded in Heaven.

Remember to read your Bible and do what it tells you. The Bible is a book that holy men wrote through the power of the Holy Spirit to tell us how to live, behave, treat each other, and what will happen in the future. We believe the Bible by faith. Words are powerful. God spoke the universe into existence. Be careful to only speak kind words and share God's word with other people.

Encourage other Christian believers.

Michael said, "August, I heard you prayed and asked Jesus to be your superhero and Lord and Savior."

August said, "Yes, I did. Jesus is my superhero. My name was written in God's book in Heaven by angels and they were happy too!"

24

Remember to pray and praise God every day for His goodness and faithfulness.

You can say, "Thank You, God, for another day. Great is Your faithfulness. Blessed are You Lord, our God, creator of the universe. I am thankful for everything and a new day. Help me to be obedient to my parents. In Jesus' (Yeshua's) name. Amen.

This prayer was written in the Bible by our heavenly Father Adonai in Numbers 6:24-26:

"May the Lord bless you and keep you. May the Lord show you his kindness. May he have mercy on you. May the Lord watch over you and give you peace." In Jesus' (Yeshua's) name. Amen.

This prayer was written in the Bible by Jesus in Matthew 6:9-13:

"Our Father in heaven, we pray that your name will always be kept holy. We pray that your kingdom will come. We pray that what you want will be done, here on earth as it is in heaven. Give us the food we need for each day. Forgive the sins we have done (when we do bad things), just as we have forgiven those who did wrong to us (those who offend us or owe us an apology). And do not cause us to be tested (help us not do bad things); but save us from the Evil One (Satan, the devil, demons, and evil people).' [The kingdom, the power, and the glory are yours forever. Amen.]"

Always remember, God forgave us so we must forgive others. God has no favorites that can get away with evil so always be good.

Anyone whose name is not found in the Book of Life will be thrown into the lake of fire. Jesus is the only way to Heaven. So, pray to receive Him and live for Him every day.

My name is Judah and my grandmother, the author of this book, prayed for God's mercy to heal me when I had a bad headache.

My testimony: There is power in praying for God's mercy for miracles in the name of Jesus.

One day, I had a bad headache and was begging my grandmother to take me to the doctor or take me to the hospital. I hate to go to the doctor, but I knew I needed help.

Grandma said, "Let me pray for you." She grabbed some anointing oil and took me to her prayer room. Grandma rubbed oil on my head and started to pray in faith asking God for mercy.

I was crying because my head hurt so bad and she started crying too. She prayed, asking God to heal me and my headache stopped. I ran downstairs and told my mother, Michelle, that God healed me after Grandma prayed.

My mom ran upstairs and told my grandmother, "Prayer works, Mom! Prayer works! Thank You, Jesus. My superhero, Jesus, has all the power, even the power to heal!"

Jesus is my superhero. I want to be like Him. Ask Him into your heart today and make Him your superhero and you can be like Him too!

John 3:16 tells us that God loved the world and everyone in it so He sent Jesus. If we believe in Jesus, we can have eternal life in Heaven.

Jesus Is My Superhero
Book Collection Series
Future Titles:

Jesus Is My Superhero:
Superpower of Miracles in Every Book of the Bible

Jesus Is My Superhero: Superpower of the Holy Rainbow

Jesus Is My Superhero: Superpower of Knowing the Future

Jesus Is My Superhero:
Superpower of Morning and Bedtime Prayers

Jesus Is My Superhero: Superpower of Hearing His Voice

Jesus Is My Superhero: Superpower of Love and Forgiveness

Jesus Is My Superhero:
Superpower of God's Blessings and Rewards

Jesus Is My Superhero:
Superpower of the Holy Spirit Makes You Special

Jesus Is My Superhero: Superpower of Thankfulness

Jesus Is My Superhero: Superpower of the Birth of a King

Jesus Is My Superhero:
Superpower of the King of Kings Return To Earth